BIRD FEATS

OF MONTANA

including
Yellowstone and
Glacier National Parks

by Deborah Richie Oberbillig

Photography by Donald M. Jones
Illustrations by James Lindquist

FARCOUNTRY
PRESS

Helena, Montana

This book is dedicated to my son, Ian, who came up with the idea for *Bird Feats*.

With great appreciation to my book reviewers:
Richard Hutto, ornithology professor, University of Montana
Steve Gniadek, wildlife biologist, Glacier National Park
Caroline Patterson, my fabulous editor at Farcountry Press

Special thanks to Missoula's Rattlesnake Elementary School teacher Catherine Schuck and her combined fourth–fifth grade class of terrific editors: Kianna Aumiller, Lauryn Byrne, Evan Carroll, Martin Chaney, Kenny Clizbe, Paul Dalenberg, Jesse Diamond, Forest Harmon, Susie Hawthorne, Paige Jones, Bo Kendall, Paige Martello, Jackson McElroy, Kate Michell, Ian Oberbillig, Jake Oetinger, Nicole Quirino, Elizabeth Swanson, Mayah Van De Wetering, and Abe Westereng

Thanks also to Janine Benyus of Biomimicry Institute, Dan Casey of American Bird Conservancy, Kate Davis of Raptors of the Rockies, Rob Domenech of Raptor View Research Institute, Kristi Dubois of Montana, Fish, Wildlife and Parks, Jay Gore of National Wildlife Federation, Matt Graves of Glacier National Park, Erick Greene of University of Montana, Sally Hejl of Glacier National Park, John Jarvis of Montana Waterfowl Foundation, Dave Oberbillig of Hellgate High School and Jay Sumner of Montana Peregrine Institute.

Black-necked stilt

Photo and Illustration Credits
Evelyn L. Bull: 33 (Vaux's swifts inside hollow tree).
Kate Davis: 9 (peregrine falcon in flight, peregrine falcon close-up).
Donald M. Jones: all bird photographs on the book's cover, back cover, and in the interior, except as noted.
Stanislaw Kinelski, Bugwood.org: 34 (fire beetle).
Hannes Lemme, Bugwood.org: 34 (beetle larvae).
James Lindquist: 6–7 (bird diagram, syrinx, hollow bones, and chicks), 9 (jet nose), 12 (bird beak), 15 (owl striking through icy crust), 16 (eagle eye and human eye), 19 (bird leg and human leg), 20 (woodpecker tongue), 26 (osprey talon), 29 (owl feather), 33 (Vaux's swift), 48 (magpie nest).
©2008 JupiterImages Corporation: 5 (Archaeopteryx), 9 (birdwatcher with binoculars), 12 (female bobolink and chicks), 14 (beetle), 15 (satellite dish), 16 (golden eagle perched on rock), 18 (walnuts), 28 (harlequin actor), 30 (kid playing harmonica).
Missouri History Museum, St. Louis: 40 (Heath cock or cock of the plains from William Clark's journal, entry date 2 March 1806).
Montana Historical Society, Helena: 37 ("Plenty Coups," photographed by Throssel, image no. 955-728).
Donald Owen, California Department of Forestry and Fire Protection, Bugwood.org: 18 (hummingbird nest).
Terry Spivey, USDA Forest Service, Bugwood.org: 47 (cliff swallow colony).
USDA Forest Service–North Central Research Station Archive, USDA Forest Service, Bugwood.org: 24 (pileated woodpecker holes in tree).
U.S. Fish and Wildlife Service: title page (trumpeter swans and white pelican), 8 (whooping crane), 9 (peregrine falcon chicks), 10 (female red-breasted merganser and male red-breasted merganser), 11 (female mallard and brood), 17 (all), 21 (white pelican in silhouette), 22 (long-billed curlew standing), 25 (American dipper), 29 (great-horned owl chicks), 36 (northern cardinal), 42 (red-winged blackbird in flight), 43 (yellow-headed blackbird feeding chicks), 44 (brown-headed cowbird), 46 (great blue heron chicks and great blue heron rookery), 47 (cliff swallow chicks).

ISBN 13: 978-1-56037-463-3
ISBN 10: 1-56037-463-2

© 2008 by Farcountry Press
Text © 2008 by Deborah Richie Oberbillig

Cover photos: Donald M. Jones
Back cover photos: Donald M. Jones

For more information on our books, write Farcountry Press, P.O. Box 5630, Helena, MT 59604; call (800) 821-3874; or visit www.farcountrypress.com.

Library of Congress Cataloging-in-Publication Data

Oberbillig, Deborah Richie, 1958-
 Bird feats of Montana : including Yellowstone and Glacier National Parks / by Deborah Richie Oberbillig.
  p. cm.
 ISBN-13: 978-1-56037-463-3 (softcover)
 ISBN-10: 1-56037-463-2 (softcover)
 1. Birds--Montana--Miscellanea. I. Title.
 QL684.M9O34 2008
 598.09786--dc22

           2007049782

Created, produced, and designed in the United States.
Printed in China.

12 11 10 09 08   1 2 3 4 5 6

Trumpeter swans

TABLE OF CONTENTS

Bobolink

White pelican

Pileated woodpecker

TABLE OF CONTENTS

Sandhill crane

BEST BIRD BRAINS

HABITATS OF THE SWIFT AND FLAME-OUS

COOLEST CALLS AND SONGS

WILDEST BEHAVIOR

NIFTIEST NESTS

Bald eagle

Clark's nutcracker

Great gray owl

A hummingbird zips by on tiny whirring wings. An owl lands without a sound. A peregrine falcon dives down toward the ground at breakneck speed, pulling up in the nick of time. Meet the *Bird Feats* champions, from the smallest bird to the fastest flier.

Judging a Champion

Ten thousand different kinds of birds fill our planet from pole to pole. Every bird, like every kid, is some kind of champion. The 40 champions in this book live in or pass through Montana. Some birds hold records we can measure, such as the biggest bill. Other birds are champions for hard-to-measure feats such as the spookiest-sounding call.

What is a Champion?

 World Champion: holds a world record, such as the fastest bird on earth

 North American Champion: holds a North American record

 Montana State Champion: holds the Montana record

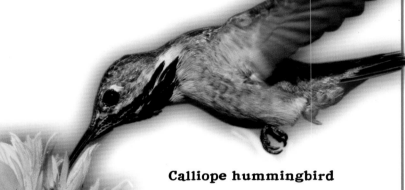

Calliope hummingbird

What is a Feat?

A feat is an amazing skill or achievement. Many bird feats are a matter of survival, such as finding food. A hummingbird has to be small to sip nectar from a flower. An owl has to fly noiselessly to catch mice. Other bird feats are connected to finding mates, building nests, or hiding from predators.

Bird Lessons

Birds have graced the Earth since the age of the dinosaurs. One of the earliest birds, *Archaeopteryx* (ar-kee-OP-ter-ix), lived 150 million years ago. Humans, by contrast, arrived only two million years ago. That's why scientists study birds to find out how we—the newcomers—can live in more environmentally friendly ways.

Archaeopteryx

What makes a bird a bird?

What does a bird have that no other animal in the world has?

Feathers!

Take a closer look at the key parts of a bird that help make this creature capable of amazing feats.

Wings

Feathers keep birds warm, are colorful, serve as camouflage, and help birds fly. Flight feathers give a bird lift and power while smaller feathers cover wings and keep air flowing smoothly.

Warm-blooded means that a bird can generate its own body heat.

Feet shapes can tell you where a bird lives and what it does. Webbed feet are for swimming; feet with two toes facing forward and two toes facing backward are for climbing trees; feet with three toes forward and one backward are for standing or for perching.

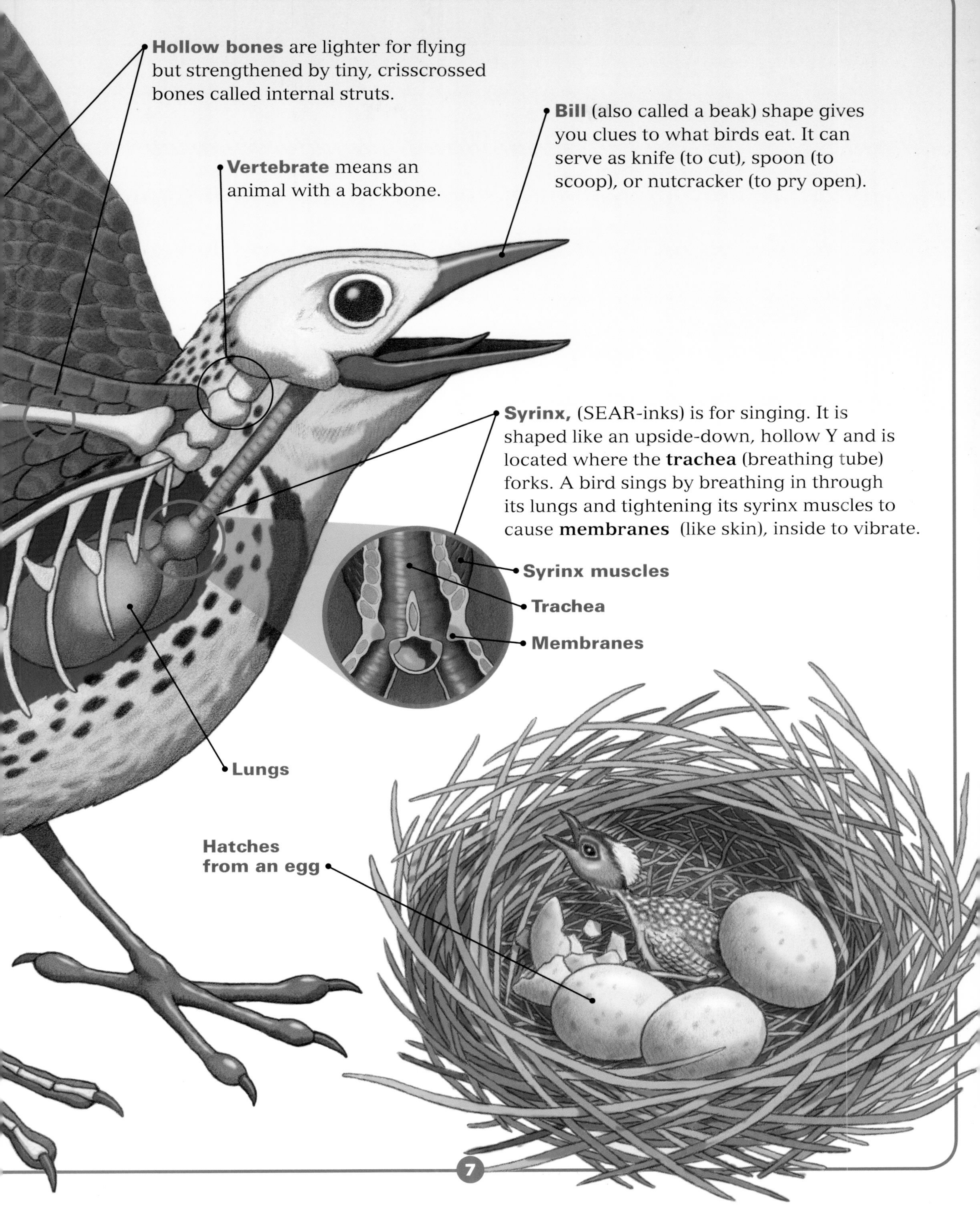

Hollow bones are lighter for flying but strengthened by tiny, crisscrossed bones called internal struts.

Vertebrate means an animal with a backbone.

Bill (also called a beak) shape gives you clues to what birds eat. It can serve as knife (to cut), spoon (to scoop), or nutcracker (to pry open).

Syrinx, (SEAR-inks) is for singing. It is shaped like an upside-down, hollow Y and is located where the **trachea** (breathing tube) forks. A bird sings by breathing in through its lungs and tightening its syrinx muscles to cause **membranes** (like skin), inside to vibrate.

Syrinx muscles

Trachea

Membranes

Lungs

Hatches from an egg

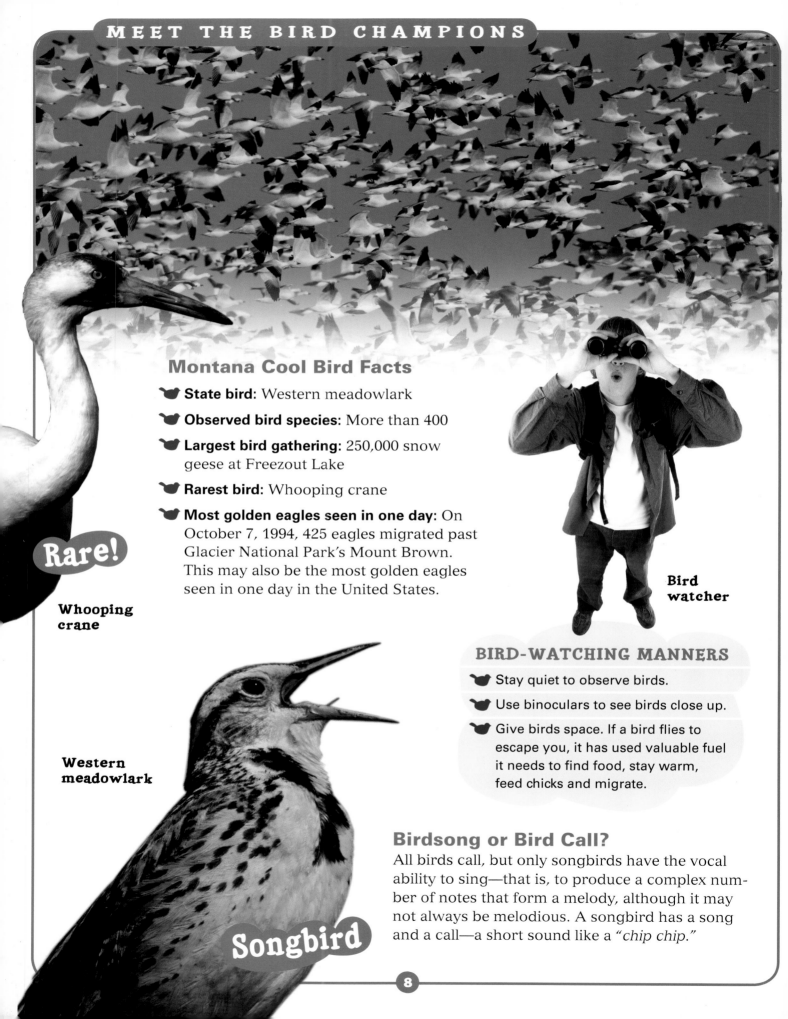

Montana Cool Bird Facts

🐦 **State bird:** Western meadowlark

🐦 **Observed bird species:** More than 400

🐦 **Largest bird gathering:** 250,000 snow geese at Freezout Lake

🐦 **Rarest bird:** Whooping crane

🐦 **Most golden eagles seen in one day:** On October 7, 1994, 425 eagles migrated past Glacier National Park's Mount Brown. This may also be the most golden eagles seen in one day in the United States.

Rare!

Whooping crane

Bird watcher

BIRD-WATCHING MANNERS

🐦 Stay quiet to observe birds.

🐦 Use binoculars to see birds close up.

🐦 Give birds space. If a bird flies to escape you, it has used valuable fuel it needs to find food, stay warm, feed chicks and migrate.

Western meadowlark

Songbird

Birdsong or Bird Call?

All birds call, but only songbirds have the vocal ability to sing—that is, to produce a complex number of notes that form a melody, although it may not always be melodious. A songbird has a song and a call—a short sound like a *"chip chip."*

FASTEST BIRD
Peregrine Falcon
Falco peregrinus

Clocking rates of more than 200 miles per hour, the **peregrine falcon** holds the animal world record for speed. Diving from the sky with a *whoosh*, the falcon will knock a duck to the ground with clenched feet or rake a songbird with a talon to snatch it mid-air. Talk about fast food!

Peregrine falcon

Peregrine Comeback

Our fastest bird came close to extinction because of the pesticide DDT. After the United States banned DDT in 1972, the peregrine still needed help. The Peregrine Fund released 6,000 falcons into the wild. Today, the peregrine is still rare but no longer endangered.

Peregrine falcon chicks

Jet Designer

Engineers designed fighter jets by studying the peregrine falcon. The bird folds its wings back to dive or "stoop," and the thin, angled wings slice through the air like knives. Even its feathers are stiff to withstand high speeds.

A peregrine has a cone in each nostril to reduce air speed so its lungs won't burst. Similarly, a jet engine has a cone that slows down the rush of incoming air to keep the jet engine from choking.

Jet engines have nose cones—as do peregrine falcons—to slow the rush of incoming air.

MONTANA BIRD-FINDING TIPS

Montana	◯◯◯
Glacier	◯◯◯ (migration)
Yellowstone	◯◯◯
Key features	Dark hood, mustache
Habitat	Cliffs, canyons, and open country
Favorite food	Birds
Seasons	Spring through fall in Montana; winter as far away as South America
Viewing spots	Cliffs overlooking rivers and lakes

◯ =EASY   ◯◯ =HARD   ◯◯◯ =HARDER

Peregrine falcon

World CHAMPION

FASTEST LEVEL FLIGHT
Red-breasted Merganser

Mergus serrator

Female red-breasted merganser

Flying straight as an arrow and just above the water, a **red-breasted merganser** (a certain kind of duck) once flew 100 mph to keep ahead of a pursuing airplane. This broke the previous record set by a canvasback duck at 72 mph! Mergansers fly fastest when chased by a predator like a bald eagle. But sprinting is tiring.

Taking off isn't easy, either. For the merganser, it's flap, splash, flap, patter, patter, flap—before liftoff. The heavy merganser has relatively small wings and has to run across the water to gather enough speed to fly.

Underwater Feats

A merganser chases fish underwater. Just as you can swim faster with a pair of flippers, all diving ducks have big, webbed feet set far back on the body for strong kicks. That's great for diving, but the position of its webbed feet makes it hard for the merganser to stay balanced when it is landing or walking.

Red-breasted merganser diving for fish

Going fishing?

MONTANA BIRD-FINDING TIPS

Montana	◯◯
Glacier	◯◯
Yellowstone	◯◯◯
Key features	Red breast, compared to common merganser's white breast
Habitat	Lakes, ponds, rivers
Favorite food	Fish
Seasons	Migrate through Montana in spring and fall.
Viewing spots	In Glacier National Park's lakes and rivers, watch for common, hooded, and red-breasted mergansers. Red-breasted mergansers nest in Canada and migrate through the park in spring and fall.

Male red-breasted merganser

10

◯ = EASY   ◯◯ = HARD   ◯◯◯ = HARDER

North American CHAMPION

HIGHEST FLIGHT
Mallard Duck

Anas platyrhynchos

Mallard duck

Quack, quack…smack! Unfortunately, the **mallard duck** that set the highest-flight record of 21,000 feet crashed into a commercial airplane over Nevada in 1962. The pilot heard a thud. Passengers in the rear felt an explosion. When the plane landed, the ground crew found a football-sized dent, a rip in the plane's tail, and a telltale mallard feather.

Into Thin Air

At 18,000 feet, there's only half as much oxygen as at sea level. You'd be gasping for breath. But a bird has an edge over you when it comes to lung power. Inside a bird's body are nine air sacs that suck air in and send it on a one-way trip through the lungs.

Male mallard duck

Female mallard duck

DUCKS, MOUNTAINS, AND AIRPLANES

200–300 feet	Typical flying altitude for migrating ducks
20,032 feet	Alaska's Mount Denali, North America's highest mountain
21,000 feet	Mallard duck collides with an airplane

Migrating Mallards

North America's most common duck, the mallard, lives just about everywhere in the United States. Most mallards, however, nest in the northern United States and Canada. The ducks that spend summers the farthest north tend to migrate the farthest south. Some mallards live in Montana all year round.

World Record Egg-Laying

Greatest number of eggs laid by a bird, one after another: 146 by a mallard duck.

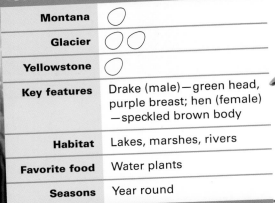

MONTANA BIRD-FINDING TIPS

Montana	◯
Glacier	◯◯
Yellowstone	◯
Key features	Drake (male)—green head, purple breast; hen (female)—speckled brown body
Habitat	Lakes, marshes, rivers
Favorite food	Water plants
Seasons	Year round

Female mallard and her chicks

◯ = EASY ◯◯ = HARD ◯◯◯ = HARDER

Montana State CHAMPION

FARTHEST SONGBIRD FLIGHT
Bobolink
Dolichonyx oryzivorus

Bubbling **bobolink** song proclaims the spring arrival of this weary traveler. Bobolinks migrate farther than any other Montana songbird—12,400 miles to South America and back. A nine-year-old female bobolink flew the equivalent of 4½ times around the earth at the equator!

Night Navigators
You won't see bobolinks migrating because they fly at night, but you might hear the musical "clink" notes overhead. Like many migratory birds, bobolinks read the stars and follow an internal compass. The compass is composed of crystals of magnetite located in the birds' beaks and between their skulls and their brains. The birds navigate by sensing the change in these magnetic crystals.

Heading South
Why fly so far? Birds migrate seasonally to find food and shelter. After nesting in the northern states, bobolinks head southward to spend winters in the grasslands of southwestern Brazil, Paraguay, or northern Argentina. Winter in Montana is summer on the other side of the equator!

Bob-bob-bob-o-linking
Bobolinks sing their name. So do chickadees. Can you think of other birds named for their sound?

Farmers and Bobolinks
Bobolinks love to nest in grassy hayfields. But that's bad news if farmers harvest before nesting season is over. If farmers wait until bobolink chicks can fly, they will protect great natural pest controls. These birds snack on insects that damage crops.

Bobolink

MONTANA BIRD-FINDING TIPS

Montana	⬭⬭
Glacier	⬭⬭⬭
Yellowstone	⬭⬭
Key features	Yellow on back of head, black breast, white rump
Habitat	Tall grass, flooded fields, grain fields
Favorite food	Insects
Seasons	Spring through summer in Montana; winter in South America

⬭ = EASY ⬭⬭ = HARD ⬭⬭⬭ = HARDER

Female bobolink and her chicks

North American CHAMPION

BEST SENSE OF SMELL
Turkey Vulture
Cathartes aura

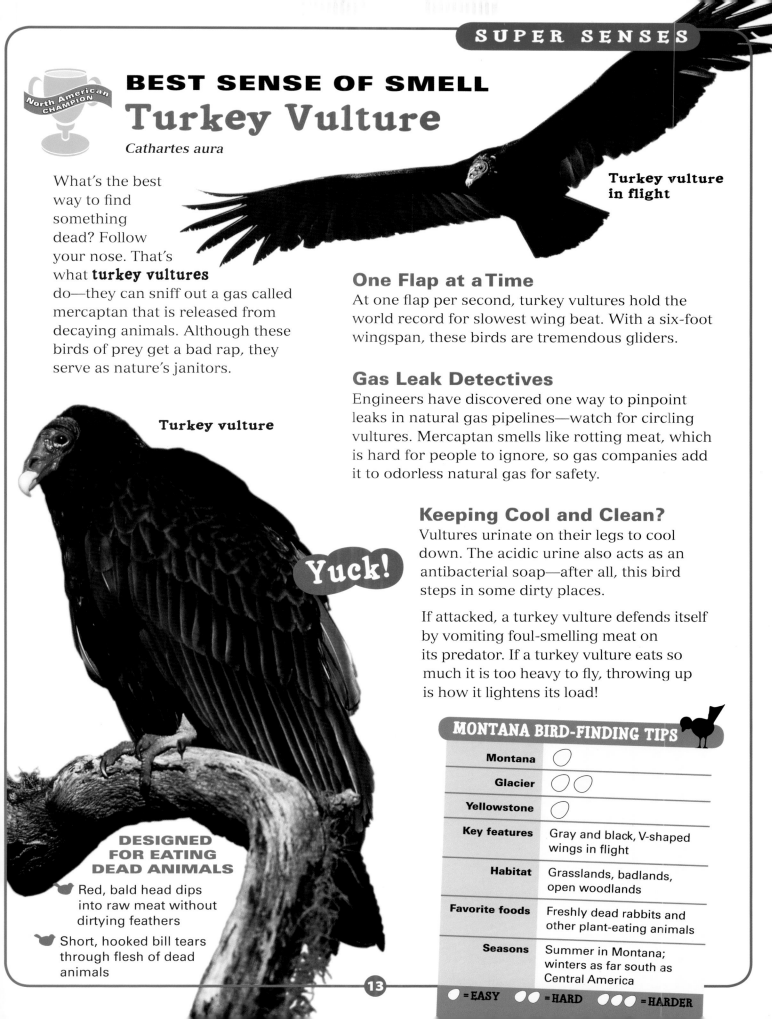

Turkey vulture in flight

What's the best way to find something dead? Follow your nose. That's what **turkey vultures** do—they can sniff out a gas called mercaptan that is released from decaying animals. Although these birds of prey get a bad rap, they serve as nature's janitors.

Turkey vulture

Yuck!

One Flap at a Time
At one flap per second, turkey vultures hold the world record for slowest wing beat. With a six-foot wingspan, these birds are tremendous gliders.

Gas Leak Detectives
Engineers have discovered one way to pinpoint leaks in natural gas pipelines—watch for circling vultures. Mercaptan smells like rotting meat, which is hard for people to ignore, so gas companies add it to odorless natural gas for safety.

Keeping Cool and Clean?
Vultures urinate on their legs to cool down. The acidic urine also acts as an antibacterial soap—after all, this bird steps in some dirty places.

If attacked, a turkey vulture defends itself by vomiting foul-smelling meat on its predator. If a turkey vulture eats so much it is too heavy to fly, throwing up is how it lightens its load!

DESIGNED FOR EATING DEAD ANIMALS

- Red, bald head dips into raw meat without dirtying feathers
- Short, hooked bill tears through flesh of dead animals

MONTANA BIRD-FINDING TIPS

Montana	◯
Glacier	◯◯
Yellowstone	◯
Key features	Gray and black, V-shaped wings in flight
Habitat	Grasslands, badlands, open woodlands
Favorite foods	Freshly dead rabbits and other plant-eating animals
Seasons	Summer in Montana; winters as far south as Central America

◯ = EASY   ◯◯ = HARD   ◯◯◯ = HARDER

BEST DUNG COLLECTOR
Burrowing Owl

Athene cunicularia

Burrowing owls have a stinky habit. During nesting season, the owls collect dung around their burrows, which attracts beetles the owls feed to their young. These daytime-feeding, ground-dwelling owls also hunt other insects, mice, and lizards.

Baiting beetles with dung sounds like a plan to bring food to the doorstep. But scientists believe this behavior developed because the owls that carried dung to their burrows raised more owlets. Those owlets, in turn, grew up to be dung collectors too.

Burrowing owl in burrow

Smelly Test
Does dung cover up the scent of eggs and protect them from predators? To test this theory, Florida researchers dug 50 burrows and placed five quail eggs (similar to owl eggs) in each hole. They spread dung around half the burrows. Predators devoured the eggs in all but one burrow. So much for that theory!

To Catch a Beetle
Ever caught a beetle with your feet? That's what a burrowing owl does. Its feet are like our hands. The owl runs along the ground and then pounces on a beetle.

Borrowed Burrow
Burrowing owls find and inhabit empty burrows, often dug by prairie dogs. The burrows can be 3 feet deep and 15 feet long.

Burrowing owl

MONTANA BIRD-FINDING TIPS

Montana	◯◯◯
Glacier	◯◯◯
Yellowstone	◯◯
Key features	Less than one foot high, long legs
Habitat	Prairie dog towns, grasslands in eastern Montana
Favorite food	Beetles
Seasons	Spring through fall in Montana; winter as far south as Central America
Viewing spots	Bear Paw Battlefield, Benton Lake National Wildlife Refuge, Charles M. Russell National Wildlife Refuge

◯ = EASY   ◯◯ = HARD   ◯◯◯ = HARDER

World CHAMPION

KEENEST HEARING
Great Gray Owl
Strix nebulosa

A **great gray owl** perches in a pine at dusk. Below, a vole (similar to a chubby mouse) tunnels under the snow. The owl turns its head, lifts off, glides down, and plunges into the white drifts, talons first. The imprint of wings in snow and speckles of blood tell the rest of the story.

How does the owl find the vole? When the vole rustles, the sound arrives in one owl ear a split second before the other, because its right ear is higher than its left ear. The owl turns its head until the sound reaches both ears at once, and then zeroes in on the location of its prey.

Facial disc

Satellite dish

Who Invented the Satellite Dish?
The bowl-shaped facial disc around an owl's eyes funnels sound to the ear slits under its feathers. A satellite dish copies the same design to gather and direct signals into your TV.

Great gray owl

A Powerful Phantom
In the northern states, Canada, and Alaska, the secretive great gray owl hunts at dusk, nighttime, and dawn. North America's tallest owl stands three feet high and weighs only three pounds, yet it can strike through icy crust thick enough to hold a 180-pound person!

Owl striking through icy crust to catch a vole

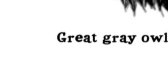

MONTANA BIRD-FINDING TIPS

Montana	◯◯◯
Glacier	◯◯◯
Yellowstone	◯◯
Key features	Large, gray, dark-ringed facial disk, yellow eyes, no ear tufts
Habitat	Forests with large trees and meadows
Seasons	Year round
Favorite foods	Pocket gophers, voles, mice, pine squirrels
Viewing spots	Yellowstone National Park's Canyon Junction and Tower–Roosevelt areas, Cascade Meadows, and Floating Island Lake

◯ = EASY ◯◯ = HARD ◯◯◯ = HARDER

North American CHAMPION

SHARPEST EYES
Golden Eagle

Aquila chrysaetos

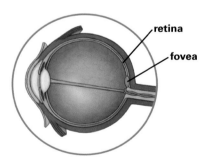

Golden eagle hunting for dinner

A **golden eagle** glides along the ragged edge of Montana's Rocky Mountain Front, scanning the grassy foothills. Far below, a jackrabbit hops into view from behind some sagebrush. The sharp-eyed eagle spots its prey and veers downward with talons outstretched.

Champion Vision Note

In 2006, Montana researcher Rob Domenech of the Raptor View Research Institute discovered that a golden eagle can spot a pigeon from miles away! The researchers placed a pigeon on a ridgetop to lure migrating golden eagles, so they could band the birds and release them. An eagle three miles away spotted the pigeon, turned around, and headed back toward the lure.

The Eagle Eye Versus the Human Eye

Here's an eagle eye compared to your eye:

Golden eagle's eye can focus at close range and far away too.

The **size** is similar, but the eagle's eye is bigger relative to its body size.

The **shape** is different. An eagle eye is roomier to allow for a larger image.

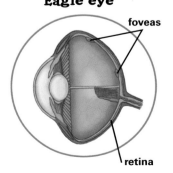

retina

fovea

Human eye

Eagle eye

foveas

retina

Fovea

This shallow bowl in the **retina** (the thin lining at the back of the eye) is the eye's focusing point. You have one **fovea**, packed full of cones sensitive to color and bright light. An eagle has two foveas —the key to its binocular vision—each with five times as many cones as you do.

MONTANA BIRD-FINDING TIPS

Montana	⬭⬭
Glacier	⬭⬭
Yellowstone	⬭⬭
Key features	Brown body, golden feathers on head.
Habitat	Open country
Favorite food	Rabbits
Seasons	Some year round in Montana; others winter as far south as central Mexico
Viewing spots	Spring/fall at Glacier National Park's Mount Brown Lookout; Rogers Pass (Hwy. 200); Bridger Mountains

⬭ = EASY ⬭⬭ = HARD ⬭⬭⬭ = HARDER

LARGEST WATERFOWL
Trumpeter Swan

Cygnus buccinator

"Nothing he had ever seen before in all his life had made him feel quite the way he felt, on that wild little pond, in the presence of those two enormous swans."

—*The Trumpet of the Swan*, E. B. White.

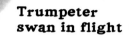

Trumpeter swan in flight

Big bird!

A **trumpeter swan** glides along Yellowstone National Park's Madison River. Graceful and big, the trumpeter swan is the largest of all wild North American waterfowl. When flying with its neck stretched out, this swan measures nearly 6 feet tall and 8 feet wide from wingtip to wingtip.

The trumpeter also weighs more than any other wild North American bird. A male swan can weigh up to 38 pounds, which is about as heavy as a four-year-old boy or girl.

Swan Songs

Trumpeter swans share lakes with the tundra swans that migrate through Montana in spring and fall. Listen to tell the swans apart. The tundra swan sounds like a high-pitched goose honking compared to the deeper, French horn-like *"ko-hoh!"* of a trumpeter swan.

What's in a Name?

A male swan is a cob; a female is a pen. A young swan is a cygnet.

Swan Survival

Elegant swan feathers once decorated ladies' hats, a deadly fashion. By 1900, trumpeter swans had almost vanished because of overhunting and habitat loss. A few survived in Yellowstone and nearby Red Rock Lakes. Gradually their numbers increased, thanks to protective laws.

MONTANA BIRD-FINDING TIPS

Montana	○○○
Glacier	○○○
Yellowstone	○ (in the right places)
Key features	White with black bill and black feet; cygnets are gray
Habitat	Lakes, slow-flowing rivers
Favorite food	Water plants
Seasons	Some year round
Viewing spots	Yellowstone National Park; Red Rock Lakes National Wildlife Refuge

○ = EASY   ○○ = HARD   ○○○ = HARDER

A pair of Trumpeter swans

North American CHAMPION

SMALLEST AND LIGHTEST
Calliope Hummingbird
Stellula calliope

Like a whirling, winged jewel, a **calliope** (cal-EYE-oh-pee) **hummingbird** is North America's smallest and lightest bird. It is also the smallest long-distance migrant in the world (5,589 miles round trip). That's a lot for a little calliope!

Hummingbirds:
The Champion Family of the Bird World

All of the world's more than 300 hummingbird species live in the western hemisphere, including the calliope, black-chinned, and rufous hummingbirds that nest in Montana.

Calliope hummingbird

HUMMER WORLD RECORDS

Fastest heartbeat	1,000 beats a minute
Fastest wing beat	90 beats per second
Fastest nectar slurper	12 slurps per second
Biggest eater	Sips more than its body weight daily
Most agile	Flies backward and upside down
Smallest nest	Smaller than a walnut
Smallest egg	1/3 of an inch (thumbnail-sized)

Hummer Heroics

A man watched a female calliope hummingbird strike a window and fall to the ground. A male calliope zoomed in, hovered above the female, trying to grip her bill and lift the slightly heavier bird. The man finally stepped in, warmed the female bird in his hands, placed her on a shrub, and watched her zoom off.

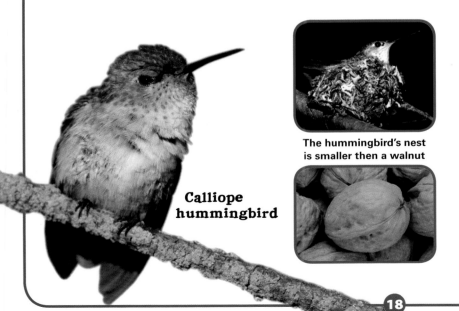

The hummingbird's nest is smaller then a walnut

Calliope hummingbird

MONTANA BIRD-FINDING TIPS

Montana	⬭⬭
Glacier	⬭⬭
Yellowstone	⬭⬭
Key features	White breast, purple starlike throat patch
Habitat	Alpine meadows, streamside forests
Favorite food	Wildflower nectar
Seasons	Summer in Montana; winter in south-central Mexico
Viewing spot	Glacier National Park's Avalanche Creek Picnic Area and Two Medicine Lake.

⬭ =EASY ⬭⬭ =HARD ⬭⬭⬭ =HARDER

Montana State CHAMPION

LONGEST LEGS
Black-necked Stilt
Himantopus mexicanus

The **black-necked stilt** earns the Montana record for longest legs in proportion to its body, second only to the world champion, the flamingo. A stilt is one-quarter body and three-quarters legs. That's like a 5-foot-tall person walking on 20-foot-long stilts.

Backwards Knees

The black-necked stilt reveals something strange about all bird legs. The knees appear to bend backward instead of forward with every step. That's because a bird's leg is like a big ankle. The "knee" is the bird's heel.

Black-necked stilt

Finding Room at the Table

Shorebirds find spots to wade at the lakeshore just like you find a place to stand in a crowded pool. The taller you are, the deeper the water you can stand in. A tall stilt can wade in six-inch-deep water and snap up bugs, while a short sandpiper has to scurry along the water's edge.

Compare Your Leg to a Bird's Leg:

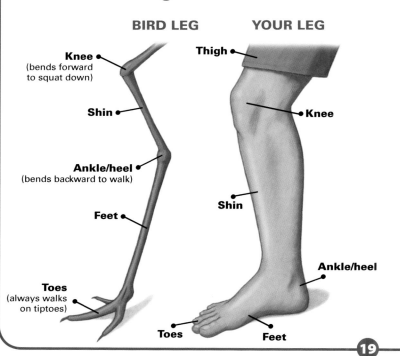

BIRD LEG

Knee (bends forward to squat down)

Shin

Ankle/heel (bends backward to walk)

Feet

Toes (always walks on tiptoes)

YOUR LEG

Thigh

Knee

Shin

Ankle/heel

Toes

Feet

MONTANA BIRD-FINDING TIPS

Montana	◯◯
Yellowstone	◯◯◯
Key features	Tuxedo of black and white, long and thin red legs, straight black bill
Habitat	Marshes, shallow lakes
Favorite foods	Water bugs, mosquito larvae, dragonfly nymphs, seeds of marsh plants
Seasons	Spring through early fall in Montana; winter in central California and coastal Texas southward
Viewing spots	Freezout Lake Wildlife Management Area, Benton Lake National Wildlife Refuge

◯ = EASY   ◯◯ = HARD   ◯◯◯ = HARDER

LONGEST TONGUE
Northern Flicker
Colaptes auratus

North American CHAMPION

Hungry flicker chicks in a nesting tree

Flick! goes the sticky tongue of the **northern flicker,** and there's one less ant in the anthill. This common woodpecker's tongue shoots out five inches—the longest tongue relative to bird size in North America.

Although all woodpeckers have long tongues with barbed points, tongue length depends on eating habits. The northern flicker's tongue is especially long because it has to snake into cracks and anthills to nab tunneling insects. If you watch this woodpecker closely while it feeds on the ground, you might see it snare ants with its sticky, saliva-covered tongue.

The woodpecker's long tongue helps it nab insects.

All Coiled Up

A woodpecker's long tongue coils up inside its skull. The flicker's tongue is so long that it curves into the base of the skull, winds up over the forehead, and attaches near the nostrils. Strong muscles shoot the tongue out and pull it back again—like a party blower or a tape measure. Tiny bones inside a casing of muscles add strength to this ant-eating tongue.

Northern flicker

The northern flicker comes in a red-shafted form that lives in western states and a yellow-shafted form that inhabits eastern and northern areas of North America.

MONTANA BIRD-FINDING TIPS

Montana	◯
Glacier	◯
Yellowstone	◯
Key features	Robin-sized, grayish, black crescent on chest
Habitat	Open woodlands, towns
Favorite food	Ants
Seasons	Year round; joined in winter by birds from Canada
Viewing spots	Tree with holes for nesting, ant hills, sides of buildings, lawns

◯ = EASY   ◯◯ = HARD   ◯◯◯ = HARDER

North American CHAMPION

BIGGEST BILL
White Pelican

Pelecanus erythrorhynchos

"A wonderful bird is the pelican. His bill can hold more than his belican!"
—Limerick by Dixon Lanier Merritt

White pelican

This expert angler scoops up fish and 3 gallons of water in an expandable pouch connected to its lower 1½-foot-long beak. Then, using special tongue muscles to tighten the pouch, the **white pelican** forces out the water and swallows the fish. Gulp!

To keep its pouch in shape, a pelican does stretching exercises—opening its mouth wide and even turning the pouch inside out by pressing it over its chest.

Two Kinds of U.S. Pelicans
White pelicans scoop up fish from western freshwater lakes and streams. Brown pelicans along the Atlantic and Pacific coasts spot fish while flying, then plunge headfirst into the water to gulp them up.

Herding Fish
White pelicans work together to drive fish into the shallow water. They encircle the trapped fish, taking turns to dip into the water to scoop them up. One pelican eats 4 pounds of fish a day, mostly suckers and carp.

Don't Swallow, Mom!
Pelican parents feed their chicks regurgitated fish (swallowed food they throw up). To eat, the baby pelican dives into the parents' giant pouch.

White pelicans looking for food

MONTANA BIRD-FINDING TIPS

Montana	◯◯
Yellowstone	◯◯
Key features	Large white body, black wingtips, orange bill. Flies with head close to body
Habitat	Lakes, rivers
Favorite food	Fish
Seasons	Spring through summer in Montana; some winter in southern California or the Gulf of Mexico
Viewing spots	Yellowstone National Park's Fishing Bridge and the Yellowstone River in Hayden Valley. The Missouri River, especially Canyon Ferry Wildlife Management Area.

● = EASY ●● = HARD ●●● = HARDER

CURVIEST DOWNTURNED BILL
Long-billed Curlew
Numenius americanus

If you've ever tried to catch grasshoppers, you know you have to pounce. A **long-billed curlew** easily plucks grasshoppers with a long bill shaped like curved tweezers.

Long-billed curlew

Curlews in the Grasses

The curlew's cry has a rising, lonesome quality—*cur-lewwww…cur-leee*. The best places to find curlews in Montana are in flat to gently rolling grasslands, near water. These birds need native grasses that aren't too tall—they can't live in plowed and planted farm fields.

Curlews love grasslands

In spring, the males perform aerial mating displays. A female usually lays four eggs in a nest on the open prairie. The chicks are downy when they hatch and are quickly able to care for themselves.

Toad Catcher?

Watch out, toad! A curlew's curved bill could be coming after you! A curlew isn't above picking up a toad, a bird's egg, or even a nestling for a meal. That long bill is great for probing mud for earthworms as well as tasty shrimp and crabs on Pacific ocean mudflats (where curlews spend the winter).

Females Win

The female curlew's bill is curvier than the male's and nine inches long—twice the length of the male's bill. Why? No one really knows yet.

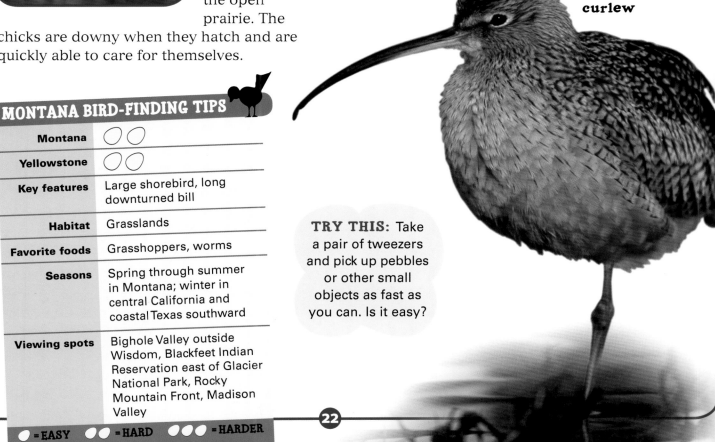

Long-billed curlew

MONTANA BIRD-FINDING TIPS

Montana	◯◯
Yellowstone	◯◯
Key features	Large shorebird, long downturned bill
Habitat	Grasslands
Favorite foods	Grasshoppers, worms
Seasons	Spring through summer in Montana; winter in central California and coastal Texas southward
Viewing spots	Bighole Valley outside Wisdom, Blackfeet Indian Reservation east of Glacier National Park, Rocky Mountain Front, Madison Valley

TRY THIS: Take a pair of tweezers and pick up pebbles or other small objects as fast as you can. Is it easy?

◯ =EASY ◯◯ =HARD ◯◯◯ =HARDER

North American
CHAMPION

CURVIEST UPTURNED BILL
American Avocet

Recurvivostra americana

American
avocet in
flight

A wading **avocet** swishes its upturned bill from side to side, just below the lake surface. The end of the avocet's bill is sensitive to touch. Clusters of sensory cells pick up the vibrations from underwater insects and shellfish, so the avocet knows when to snap its bill together to catch a meal. Birds can even sense an earthquake or tsunami—a tidal wave—before we can, because of these sensory cells that can be located on their bills (like avocets), tongues, and legs.

American
avocet

Upturned Versus Downturned Bill

Which bill shape works better for stirring insects up to the surface? To find out, fill up a bowl with water. Add some peppercorns or dry beans. Hold a spoon as if you were eating soup. Now, swing it back and forth evenly and deeply through the water, avocet-style. Then, turn the spoon over, and try swishing it (like a downturned bill).

Teamwork Pays Off

Avocets work together to herd aquatic insects. You may see them parading through the shallows with their heads lowered, sweeping their bills like scythes.

American avocets herding fish

MONTANA BIRD-FINDING TIPS

Montana	⬭⬭	
Glacier	⬭⬭⬭	
Yellowstone	⬭⬭	
Key features	Cinnamon head and neck with black-and-white wings, long legs, upturned black bill	
Habitat	Shallow lakes, marshes.	
Favorite foods	Water insects, crustaceans.	
Seasons	Spring through summer in Montana; winter along the coast in California and Mexico	

⬭ = EASY　⬭⬭ = HARD　⬭⬭⬭ = HARDER

Montana State CHAMPION

STRONGEST BILL
Pileated Woodpecker
Dryocopus pileatus

Holes made by a hungry pileated woodpecker

Whack! Using its head as a hammer, a **pileated woodpecker** strikes a tree with its bill, and wood chips fly. If you used your head as a hammer, you'd have to hit a wall at 16 miles per hour to match the impact. Ouch! To top it off, Montana's largest woodpecker hammers up to 20 times per second or 1,200 times per minute!

The woodpecker's chisel-shaped bill delivers swift and straight blows into decaying trees. The wood splinters apart to reveal juicy ants and grubs that the woodpecker snags with its long, barbed tongue.

TIME YOURSELF:
How many times can you tap a pencil on a desk in one minute?

Carpenter Safety
The pileated woodpecker is built for carpentry. A thick skull and spongy cartilage at the beak's base absorb the shock of hammering. Strong muscles attach the upper and lower jaws to the skull and relay the force of the blows to the back of the skull. Tufts of feathers shield the bird's nostrils from sawdust.

Whack!

Pileated woodpecker

Making a Mark
Big, rectangular holes in a tree are a sure sign of a feeding pileated woodpecker. Nesting cavities are roughly triangular and just big enough for birds to squeeze in and out of. A male and female will work together for about a month to dig out a nesting cavity, which can be two feet deep inside a dead tree.

MONTANA BIRD-FINDING TIPS

Montana	◯◯	
Glacier	◯◯	
Key features	Crow-sized, red crest, black and white striped face, loud laughing call	
Habitat	Forests with large trees and snags (dead trees)	
Favorite food	Carpenter ants	
Seasons	Year round	

◯ = EASY ◯◯ = HARD ◯◯◯ = HARDER

BEST UNDERWATER WALKER
American Dipper

Cinclus mexicanus

American dipper

This bouncy songbird walks on the stream bottom, wades in shallow water, and swims down to depths of 20 feet to catch caddis fly larvae. To keep from bobbing to the surface, the **dipper** grasps rocks with its strong toes and flaps its stubby wings.

Skin Diver minus Flippers

Like a skin diver, the dipper is equipped for cold water, except the bird lacks webbed feet. Instead, the dipper paddles its wings like flippers.

American dipper dipping underwater for caddis fly larvae

Nature's wet suit	A dipper stays snug with twice as many outer feathers as other songbirds (more than 6,000 feathers over a thick down undercoat).
Waterproof feathers	All birds use their bills to "preen" or clean and waterproof their feathers by spreading oil from a special gland at their tails' base. Dippers' oil glands are ten times larger than other songbirds'.
Diver's mask	All birds have a third clear eyelid (called a nictitating membrane) beneath the upper and lower eye-lids, which can be drawn across the eye like a diver's mask.
Nose plugs	A movable flap covers its nostrils underwater.
Snorkel	A dipper can stay underwater for 30 seconds or so. No snorkel needed!

Dippers under Footbridges
Look for dippers dipping on rocks or for their round mossy nests under foot-bridges. Listen for their lovely liquid song. Look for their "whitewash" or poop on rocks in mountain streams.

MONTANA BIRD-FINDING TIPS

Montana	⬭
Glacier	⬭
Yellowstone	⬭
Key features	Steely gray songbird
Habitat	Rocky, cold, clean streams
Favorite foods	Caddis fly larvae, stonefly nymphs
Seasons	Year round

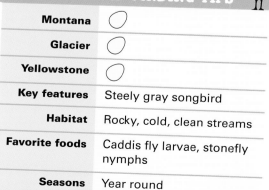

⬭ =EASY ⬭⬭ =HARD ⬭⬭⬭ =HARDER

BEST FISHHOOKS

Osprey

Pandion haliaetus

An **osprey** hovers above the Flathead River, focusing on a rainbow trout. Then, in a blur of feathers, it whizzes down and splashes into the water feet first, talons snapping shut. The osprey rises, carrying the dripping fish tailfirst to cut down on wind resistance.

Osprey

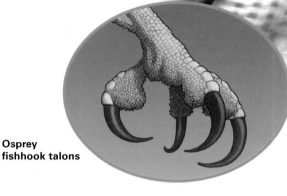

Osprey fishhook talons

Spiny Pads

If your palms were spiny and as rough as sandpaper, you'd get a better grip on a football. Similarly, the osprey can hang onto a slippery fish, because it has both sharp talons and spines (called spicules) on the pads of its toes.

The Amazing Reversible Toe

The osprey, like the owl, has a reversible outer toe. When perching on a limb, the osprey keeps three toes in front and one in back for stability. To hold a fish, the osprey rotates its outer toe back so it has two toes in front and two in back.

Gripping Sticks

Talons are handy for nest-building. A male osprey will break off a dead branch in midflight to add to a treetop stick nest or osprey platform. Sometimes, ospreys choose deadly nest decorations, such as plastic baling twine or nylon fishing line, which can strangle nestlings and adult birds.

WHAT YOU CAN DO:
- Pick up twine and fishing line.
- Litter isn't just ugly—it can be deadly for birds.

MONTANA BIRD-FINDING TIPS

Montana	○	
Glacier	○	
Yellowstone	○	
Key features	Long slim wings, white head, dark eye stripe
Habitat	Lakes, rivers, ponds, marshes
Favorite food	Fish—particularly suckers and squawfish
Seasons	Spring through fall in Montana, winter as far south as Central and South America

○ = EASY   ○○ = HARD   ○○○ = HARDER

Osprey carrying a fish to its nest

BEST INVISIBILITY CLOAK
White-tailed Ptarmigan
Lagopus leucurus

Like Harry Potter and his cloak, this bird has the invisibility trick down. In winter, the **white-tailed ptarmigan** (TAR-mih-gan) grows white feathers to vanish within its snowy home. When the snow melts in spring, the invisibility cloak no longer works. This is the time for the ptarmigan to molt (shed) its white feathers and grow brown and gray ones. Now, the ptarmigan will easily disappear again among the rocks and bushes of its steep mountain home.

Timing is Everything
How does a ptarmigan know when to change color? Like all birds, they molt their feathers a certain number of days after the end of the nesting season. The white feathers grow in time to match the winter snow.

Why Camouflage?
Ptarmigans spend their lives in harm's way, feeding on the ground. Camouflage in winter and summer protects ptarmigans from being seen by hungry predators, such as coyotes, grizzly bears, and eagles.

A ptarmigan in winter blends into the snow

A ptarmigan in summer matches the mountain slopes

WINTER WEAR
What Montana mammal wears winter white and natural snowshoes?

(Answer: The snowshoe hare.)

Bird Snowshoes
Stiff white feathers cloak the ptarmigan's feet and legs for warmth. The feathers also act as fluffy snowshoes that help keep the bird on top of the snowdrifts.

White-tailed ptarmigan molting

MONTANA BIRD-FINDING TIPS

Montana	○○
Glacier	○○
Key features	Small grouse, white tail year round
Habitat	Alpine
Favorite foods	Leaves, needles, buds, seeds
Seasons	Year round
Viewing spot	Glacier National Park and northwestern Montana above timberline

○ =EASY ○○ =HARD ○○○ =HARDER

MOST CLOWNLIKE BIRD
Harlequin Duck
Histrionicus histrionicus

A harlequin male duck glides along the river

Harlequin male duck

This rare duck is named **harlequin** (HAR-le-kwin) after a kind of Italian clown that dressed in diamond-patterned tights and performed in theaters. Its scientific name, *Histrionicus,* is the Latin word for an actor. Do you think the duck's feather pattern looks like the original harlequin? Or it is just a little clownish?

Shhh!

Do Not Disturb!
These ducks are shy and can be easily frightened. Please watch with binoculars from a safe distance.

Harlequin actor

Splashy Camouflage
Those clownish white spots and streaks on a male harlequin look like splashes of frothing water in a mountain stream, which is a harlequin's habitat. By contrast, the female is brown, with just one white spot on the side of her head. The drab coloring keeps her hidden from predators while she is incubating eggs in her nest, which is often tucked in a hollow tree or between rocks.

Female and male harlequin ducks

MONTANA BIRD-FINDING TIPS

Montana	◯◯◯
Glacier	◯
Yellowstone	◯◯◯
Key features	Diving duck; male: dark body with white bars, long tail
Habitat	Whitewater, rough mountain streams
Favorite food	Caddis fly larvae
Seasons	Summer in Montana; winter on the Pacific coast
Viewing spots	Look for harlequins in Glacier National Park in May and June along the waterfalls on upper McDonald Creek. By late June, male harlequins head to the coast, leaving females to raise the chicks. By mid-September, all harlequins have flown west to the Pacific coast.

◯ = EASY ◯◯ = HARD ◯◯◯ = HARDER

MOST SILENT FLIGHT
Great-Horned Owl

Bubo virginianus

A family gathers around a campfire under starry skies. Above them, a massive **great-horned owl** takes off from a tree and flaps into the night, fading away like a ghost. No one hears it. All owls share the world record for most silent flight.

Feather Feat

The secret to the ghostly owl's flight lies in the bird's fringed feathers and velvety wings. Air passes over these sound-silencing wings without creating noisy turbulence.

🐦 Fringe on the trailing edge of the feather calms rough air.

🐦 Comblike structures on the leading edge of the feather breaks up airflow.

Great-horned owl chicks

Planes Like Owls

Engineers are studying owl feathers to design quieter planes during takeoff and landing. Some day you might see plane wings with fringes and a velvety coating on the landing gear!

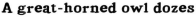

A great-horned owl dozes

Great Horns?

Tufts on an owl aren't horns or ears. They are actually feathers. Those tufts, plus the mottled feathers, disguise the owl to look like part of the tree where it snoozes during the day. The great-horned owl is nocturnal, which means that it's active at night.

TRY THIS:

Take two pieces of rope. Unravel one so fibers form a fringe. Keep the other rope intact. Swing the two pieces in the air.

Which rope is quieter?

MONTANA BIRD-FINDING TIPS

Montana	⚪⚪	
Glacier	⚪⚪	
Yellowstone	⚪⚪	
Key features	Large owl—ear tufts, yellow eyes, deep hooting call.	
Habitat	Forests, open meadows	
Favorite foods	Small mammals like rabbits, mice, gophers	
Seasons	Year round	

⚪ = EASY   ⚪⚪ = HARD   ⚪⚪⚪ = HARDER

BEST SOUND EFFECTS
Wilson's Snipe
Gallinago delicata

The **Wilson's snipe** skydives with its outer tail feathers spread out, one on each side. As the bird plummets earthward, the tail feathers vibrate, creating a *"woo-woo-woo-woo"* sound that grows louder as the snipe gains speed.

In April and May, male and female snipes join spring courtship flights over wetlands at dusk, dawn, or on moonlit nights. Birds circle into the sky to nearly 300 feet, tails spread to make a twittering noise. At the top of their climb, they fold their wings back and dive at nearly 25 to 50 mph, and the sound changes to the *"woo-woo-woo"* that birders call "winnowing." Then, like daredevil pilots, they pull up and do it again.

Nest Defender
Once a male and female have mated, they no longer perform musical flights. The female selects a nesting site on a mound, close to a bog or wet pasture. The male continues diving to defend his territory.

Wilson's snipe

Like a Harmonica
When you blow through a harmonica, the reeds inside the instrument vibrate, just like the snipe's vibrating tail feathers.

Wilson's snipe

The secretive snipe's flexible bill has sensory pits at the tip so it can feel for insects and worms.

MONTANA BIRD-FINDING TIPS

Montana	◯◯	
Glacier	◯◯	
Yellowstone	◯	
Key features	Stocky body, short legs, long bill, striped back	
Habitat	Damp, grassy fields	
Favorite foods	Worms, insect larvae	
Seasons	Spring through fall in Montana; winter most migrate south, some stay year round	

◯ = EASY   ◯◯ = HARD   ◯◯◯ = HARDER

BEST MEMORY
Clark's Nutcracker

Nucifraga columbiana

"*Kraak, Kra-a-ak!*" A bold gray and black bird may land on your picnic table to snatch a crumb—that's a likely way to meet the **Clark's nutcracker** in the Rocky Mountains. By fall, however, this bird is busy collecting pine seeds. One nutcracker can gather 30,000 seeds and bury them in 7,500 spots spread out over miles. Months later, the bird can find 70 percent of its winter food supplies—called **caches**—even under snow.

Remember this?

Want to sharpen your memory? Take a tip from a pro. A Clark's nutcracker buries its seeds next to a rock or some recognizable object. Then, it makes a mental note. Can you make a map in your head to remember where you've hidden your secret treasures?

The Clark's nutcracker was named for William Clark of the Lewis and Clark Expedition, who first described this bird in 1805.

Tree Planter

On a mountain ridge, a Clark's nutcracker uses its razor-sharp bill to pry open the sealed cone of a whitebark pine. After gathering approximately 70 of the oily, nutritious seeds in a specialized throat pouch, the nutcracker flies off to bury its booty, a few seeds at a time, one inch deep in the ground.

All winter, the nutcracker digs up seeds to eat. Red squirrels and grizzly bears also eat whitebark seeds. The squirrels harvest the cones from the treetops and store them in piles called middens. Grizzly bears munch the cones from the squirrel middens. Nutcrackers dig up their hidden seeds under the snow over the winter, but the leftovers sprout into seedlings.

Clark's
nutcracker

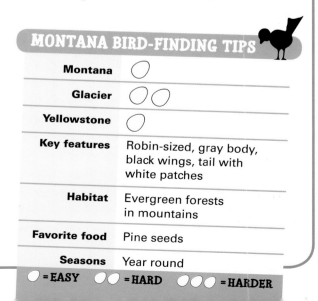

MONTANA BIRD-FINDING TIPS

Montana	◯	
Glacier	◯ ◯	
Yellowstone	◯	
Key features	Robin-sized, gray body, black wings, tail with white patches	
Habitat	Evergreen forests in mountains	
Favorite food	Pine seeds	
Seasons	Year round	

◯ = EASY   ◯◯ = HARD   ◯◯◯ = HARDER

SMARTEST
Common Raven
Corvus corax

Have you been outsmarted by a **raven?** It happened to me. Once, a raven swooped down, tore a page out of my book and flew off. I'd left the book lying open at my campsite for only a minute. Naturally, the raven seized the page I hadn't read yet!

Ravens share their smarts with other members of the Corvid family—crows, jays, nutcrackers, and magpies. But ravens are the brainiest, according to bird scientist, Bernd Heinrich. He found that when a raven locates a dead animal like a moose, the bird flies back to the roost to share the good news and then leads the flock to the feast. Sharing information helps the flock survive.

Common raven sharing some good news

Yellowstone's Wolf Bird
Ravens and wolves play and work together. Yellowstone National Park researchers have watched a raven hop up to a wolf pup and gently tug its tail. Ravens follow wolves on the hunt to share fresh elk meat. In turn, wolves follow the ravens to guide the pack to prey.

Playing in the Wind
There's nothing like a good storm to send ravens flying—looping, diving, twisting, and zooming in the gusts. Ravens are smart and playful.

Common ravens

Yummy!

Ravens feed on dead animals, eggs, baby birds, insects, fruit, and even picnic lunches. Always pick up crumbs and keep a clean camp.

MONTANA BIRD-FINDING TIPS

Montana	◯
Glacier	◯
Yellowstone	◯
Key features	Larger than crows, black, shaggy neck feathers, wedge-shaped tail, deep croaking call
Habitat	Mountains to prairies, prefers cliffs for nesting
Favorite food	Dead animals
Seasons	Year round

◯ = EASY   ◯◯ = HARD   ◯◯◯ = HARDER

HOLLOW TREE CHAMPION
Vaux's Swift

Chaetura vauxi

Night descends upon the forest. **Vaux's** (pronounced like "foxes" with a V) **swifts** pour down from the sky like smoke and spiral into a hollow cedar tree. Safely inside, the birds cling to the tree trunk and sleep. As the next day warms, the swifts leave again to spend their waking hours on the wing.

Apodidae (A-PODE-ih-dee), the Latin name for the swift family, means "without feet." Swifts have feet, but they are so small and weak the birds cannot perch. Instead they have claws on their toes for hanging onto vertical surfaces and stiff tail feathers for clasping onto walls.

Vaux's swifts hanging onto the inside of a hollow tree.

SWIFT RECORDS

Smallest	The Vaux's swift is North America's tiniest swift at 4½ inches long
Shortest legs	Swifts have almost non-existent legs
Most aerial	Swifts spend more time in the air flying than any other land bird

Hammock Nest
Swifts hang their nests in tree cavities, which requires nature's version of superglue. They use their sticky saliva to superglue twigs together and to glue the nest onto the trunk. The final touch? A soft lining of evergreen needles.

Hungry Mouths to Feed
A swift parent often flies with its mouth open, trapping tiny insects to deliver to as many as seven hungry chicks.

Vaux's swift

MONTANA BIRD-FINDING TIPS

Montana	◯ ◯ (Western only)
Glacier	◯ ◯
Key features	Torpedo-shaped body, crescent-shaped slim wings
Habitat	Forests with dead or hollow trees
Favorite foods	Flying insects, ballooning spiders
Seasons	Spring through fall in Montana; winter as far south as Venezuela, South America
Viewing spots	Western Montana, especially along Glacier National Park's Trail of the Cedars and in Missoula's Greenough Park

◯ = EASY   ◯◯ = HARD   ◯◯◯ = HARDER

MOST FIRE-LOVING
Black-backed Woodpecker

Picoides arcticus

Boom! Crack! Lightning strikes. A Douglas fir bursts into flames. Sparks fly and a summer wildfire takes off across the dry Montana forest. By the next year, the charred trees will echo with the *tap-tap-tap* of the most fire-loving bird, the **black-backed woodpecker.** This bird even has sooty black feathers to blend in with burned trees.

Like the story of the mythical phoenix that has the magical power to die in flames and rise from the ashes, the black-backed woodpecker shows up after a forest fire. The woodpecker is attracted to the smoky woods by the promise of a delicious snack: a kind of wood-boring beetle called a fire beetle.

Fire beetle

Beetle Mania

Fire beetles are the black-backed woodpeckers' favorite quarry in trees. These beetles fly straight for burned, smoking trees, which they can detect nearly 50 miles away. There they mate, lay eggs, and hatch into white grubs that bore into the trees until the larvae become adults. Thousands of these larvae are speared on woodpecker tongues. One black-backed woodpecker can eat 13,500 beetle larvae in a year.

Beetle larvae

The Hotter the Better

Not all fires burn the same. Some fires only scorch trees. Intense, hot fires are the ones that attract the beetles eaten by black-backed woodpeckers.

MONTANA BIRD-FINDING TIPS

Montana	◯◯◯
Glacier	◯◯
Yellowstone	◯◯◯
Key features	Black back, black-and-white barred sides, white belly, yellow-capped male.
Habitat	Recently burned forests, with Douglas fir, western larch, and subalpine fir trees
Favorite food	Beetle larvae
Seasons	Year round

◯ =EASY ◯◯ =HARD ◯◯◯ =HARDER

BEST RAPPER
Lazuli Bunting

Passerina amoena

Though they may not sound like it to us, **lazuli** (LAZZ-yo-lie) **bunting** males are nature's rappers. In fact, every male composes his own unique song to attract a mate or defend a territory.

Young lazuli buntings pick up song ideas from older males in the shrubs. The birds take these musical tidbits and use them to invent their own songs. So, while all male bunting songs are different, you can trace the birds back to the shrubs where they grew up.

Every male lazuli bunting composes his own song.

Red's Story

Dr. Erick Greene, a University of Montana biology professor, and his graduate students observed a particularly talented rapper, which they nicknamed "Red." Yearling male buntings crowded around him and copied his songs, as if they wanted to become Red himself. What did Red do? He changed his song and once again was the neighborhood star.

Lazuli bunting

A Fresh Air Recording Studio

Greene and his graduate students have spent years tromping up and down Mount Sentinel in Missoula, holding out long microphones to record lazuli bunting tunes.

In the studio, they slowed the songs way down and played them back. They found that buntings are rappers, and that one male bunting's song, slowed down, sounded like this silly jingle: "The worms crawl in, the worms crawl out, the worms play pinochle on your snout…."

MONTANA BIRD-FINDING TIPS

Montana	○○	
Glacier	○○	
Yellowstone	○○	
Key features	Small songbird; breeding male—blue head and back, red chest, white belly; female and nonbreeding male—dull brown	
Habitat	Brushy hillsides, streamsides, and open woods	
Favorite foods	Insects, seeds	
Seasons	Spring through summer in Montana; winter in western Mexico	

○ = EASY   ○○ = HARD   ○○○ = HARDER

STATE BIRD

SWEETEST SPRING SONG
Western Meadowlark
Sternella neglecta

Western meadowlark singing

If sunshine could be transformed into music, it would sound like a **western meadowlark.** No wonder six states—Kansas, Montana, Nebraska, North Dakota, Oregon, and Wyoming—have chosen this bard of spring as their state bird. Montana schoolchildren voted for the western meadowlark as the state bird in 1930, and the next year the state legislature made it official.

Why Sing in Spring?
A male meadowlark perches on a fence-post, tips back his head, and sings to let other males know that he has claimed the field. Males arrive in March, several weeks before the females. This gives the males time to set up nesting territories.

You Say Tomato, I Say Tomahto
Western and eastern meadowlarks look almost identical and their ranges overlap in the middle of the United States. But there are subtle differences. The eastern meadowlark's song is higher, clearer, and less complex than the western meadowlark's seven- to ten-note song.

Sweet spring

Western meadowlark

Did you know?
The western meadowlark is the second most popular state bird.

Which is the first?

(Answer: The northern cardinal.)

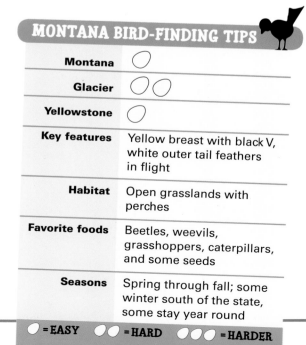

MONTANA BIRD-FINDING TIPS

Montana	◯
Glacier	◯◯
Yellowstone	◯
Key features	Yellow breast with black V, white outer tail feathers in flight
Habitat	Open grasslands with perches
Favorite foods	Beetles, weevils, grasshoppers, caterpillars, and some seeds
Seasons	Spring through fall; some winter south of the state, some stay year round

◯ = EASY   ◯◯ = HARD   ◯◯◯ = HARDER

BEST ALARM CALL
Black-capped Chickadee
Poecile atricapilla

Try to sneak up on a **black-capped chickadee.** This chatty observer immediately alerts other birds with its alarm call of *"chick-a-dee-dee."* It might be saying, *"Human coming this way! No big deal."* If it was a pygmy owl or sharp-shinned hawk, however, the message might be, *"Chick-a-dee-dee-dee-dee-dee-dee!"* or, *"Danger! Predator! Let's drive it away now!"*

Chick-a dee-dee-dee-dee-dee-dee

Black-capped chickadee alerting others

Black-capped chickadee enjoying a tasty caterpillar

What Do Those *Dee-Dee-Dees* Mean?
University of Montana researchers and bird educator Kate Davis of Raptors of the Rockies teamed up to decode these alarm messages:

"Chick-a-deeee-deee" indicated a low-threat, big bird of prey, such as a great-horned owl or a red-tailed hawk.

"Chick-a-dee-dee-dee-dee-dee-dee" indicated a high-threat small bird of prey, such as a pygmy owl or a sharp-shinned hawk.

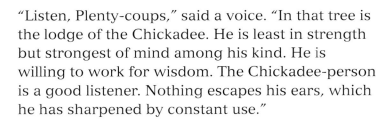

Chief Plenty Coups

Chief Plenty Coups' Spirit Guide
In *Plenty-coups, Chief of the Crows*, Frank B. Linderman describes how Montana's famous leader of the Crow Indians, Chief Plenty Coups (1848 to 1932), found his spirit guide, the chickadee, in a dream:

"Listen, Plenty-coups," said a voice. "In that tree is the lodge of the Chickadee. He is least in strength but strongest of mind among his kind. He is willing to work for wisdom. The Chickadee-person is a good listener. Nothing escapes his ears, which he has sharpened by constant use."

MONTANA BIRD-FINDING TIPS

Montana	◯
Glacier	◯
Yellowstone	◯
Key features	Black cap, black bib, white cheeks
Habitat	Forest edges, nests in tree cavities
Favorite foods	Caterpillars, seeds
Seasons	Year round

◯ = EASY   ◯◯ = HARD   ◯◯◯ = HARDER

SPOOKIEST CALL
Common Loon

Gavia immer

Common loon

"Whoooo areeeee youuuu?" This ghostly wail curls across a lake, followed by the quavering laughter of Montana's spookiest bird. When your shivers stop, listen to the **loon's** four different calls.

The **hoot** is the soft, single note of a parent reassuring a chick. Loon chicks often snuggle on their parents' backs to keep warm and safe.

The **wail** is a questioning call, checking on the identity and whereabouts of other loons. The *"Whooo are you?"* rises, lingers, and then fades away.

Female loon and her chick

The **tremolo** is the loon's crazy, five-note musical laughter it utters when a boat comes too close to a nest.

The **yodel** starts low, climbs, and is followed by a frenzied tumble of notes. Male loons will yodel to challenge each other or to scare away an intruder.

A male loon will rise out of the water, yodel and flap its wings to scare away an intruder

Montana: A Loon Hot Spot

More loons nest on western Montana lakes than anywhere west of the Mississippi River, but they are not common. There are fewer than 200 loons in Montana; one-fifth of them are in Glacier National Park.

STAY CLEAR of loon nesting areas (usually marked by buoys as off limits). Give all loons plenty of room. Never chase any water bird in a boat.

MONTANA BIRD-FINDING TIPS

Montana	◯◯
Glacier	◯◯
Yellowstone	◯
Key features	Black head, white-flecked feathers, black back and necklace, red eyes
Habitat	Small, quiet western Montana lakes, migrate through many parts of the state
Favorite food	Fish
Seasons	Spring through fall in Montana; most winter on the Pacific coast, some winter on Montana lakes
Viewing spots	Lakes in Glacier National Park and in the Seeley-Swan Valley

◯ = EASY ◯◯ = HARD ◯◯◯ = HARDER

Common loon on nest

HIGHEST LEAP
Sandhill Crane

Grus canadensis

Two **sandhill cranes** face each other in a lush meadow. They bow and open their wide wings. Next, they lift up their heads, thrust their wings down, and leap 10 feet into the air—twice as high as the best ballet dancers can jump.

Sandhill crane in flight

SANDHILL SNIPPETS

- North American sandhill and whooping cranes are part of fifteen crane species worldwide; seven are endangered.
- Crow Indians believed migrating songbirds rode on the backs of cranes.
- Greater sandhill cranes can fly 365 miles nonstop, averaging 38 miles per hour.
- Sandhills bugle from windpipes shaped like French horns.
- Male and female cranes share the jobs of nest-tending and raising the young, called "colts."

Why Leap and Dance?

Sandhill cranes mate for life. To renew their bonds, the pairs dance, toss sticks in the air, and sing duets. All cranes leap to let off steam, too. Crane communities get along well together, perhaps because they spend so much time dancing. The Latin word for crane, *grus,* forms the root of the English word, "congruence," which means agreement. Certainly, cranes seem to live in agreement.

Sandhill crane leaping

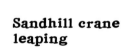

MONTANA BIRD-FINDING TIPS

Montana	◯◯
Glacier	◯◯◯
Yellowstone	◯◯
Key features	4 feet tall, long legs and neck, slender pointed bill, gray with bright red crown
Habitat	Wet meadows, marshes, fields
Favorite foods	Grains, seeds, sometimes insects
Seasons	Spring through summer; winter in New Mexico
Viewing spots	Yellowstone National Park's Fountain Flats (between Madison and Old Faithful) or Wildlife Overlook (between Fishing Bridge and Canyon). Pairs build mounded nests in wet meadows in late April and early May.

◯ = EASY   ◯◯ = HARD   ◯◯◯ = HARDER

LONGEST DANCE
Sage Grouse
Centrocercus urophasianus

What's the biggest and longest bird dance competition in Montana? The **sage grouse** boogie! It takes place at dawn from mid-March to mid-April in clearings called *leks* (the Swedish word for play). As many as 100 male sage grouse boogie to impress the female grouse.

The sage grouse strut goes like this: The male grouse fans his spiky tail, puffs up his white chest feathers, and swaggers up to his competitor. He stomps the ground, inflates two olive-green air sacs hidden in his fluffy chest, draws back his head, and—pop! The sacs deflate. This two-step stomp inspired ceremonial dances of Plains Indian tribes.

Sage grouse fanning his tail

Favorite Dance Hall
The birds return to the same lek every year. After the females mate, they fly off to nest. The males keep dancing until the spring ritual ends. Then at last, the exhausted birds leave the lek to regain their strength. Some leks are more than 100 years old.

William Clark's sketch of the sage grouse

Cock of the Plains
Captain Meriwether Lewis first saw the sage grouse, which he called the "cock of the plains," in 1806 near the Marias River in Montana. He was observing North America's largest grouse, found only on western prairies with sagebrush.

Sage grouse lek

MONTANA BIRD-FINDING TIPS

Montana	◯◯
Yellowstone	◯◯◯
Key features	Chicken-sized, blotchy brown, male—larger with a white chest and black throat
Habitat	Sagebrush
Favorite food	Sagebrush
Seasons	Year round
Viewing spots	Big Hole Valley, Charles M. Russell National Wildlife Refuge near Lewistown

◯ = EASY   ◯◯ = HARD   ◯◯◯ = HARDER

BRAVEST PARENT
Killdeer

Charadrius vociferus

A Killdeer dragging its wing

These shorebird parents risk their lives daily for their chicks. A **killdeer** runs directly into harm's way, dragging its wing to lure a hungry fox or raccoon away from the nest. The bird cries, *"Kill-deer, Kill-deer!"* as if to say, *"I'm injured! Chase me!"* Once the chicks are safe, the killdeer flies off.

Killdeer often choose perilous places to nest. They like open spots with little or no grass so they can see danger coming. You'll find them in gravel parking lots, golf courses, pastures, and even in playing fields.

Chase me!

Egg and Chick Care

Killdeer eggs can heat up too much on a hot day. The parents soak their feathers in water so when they sit on the nest, they cool the speckled eggs (usually four). After 24 to 26 days, the killdeer chicks hatch in June, ready to scamper out of harm's way or blend into the pebbly ground with their brown mottled feathers.

Fluff and Bluff

The broken wing act doesn't work with a clumsy horse or cow that is about to step on a nest or a chick. In this situation, the killdeer fluffs up its feathers and charges the giant. The surprised animal will usually step aside.

Distraction Displays

Many ground-nesting birds fake broken wings to lead predators away from eggs or chicks. When you're out hiking in the grasslands, you might see a sparrow dragging a wing, too.

Killdeer nesting

MONTANA BIRD-FINDING TIPS

Montana	◯
Glacier	◯
Yellowstone	◯
Key features	Robin-sized, two black bands on chest
Habitat	Open lands, grazed pastures, mudflats, gravel bars along streams
Favorite foods	Insects, spiders, ticks
Seasons	Some year round; others winter south of Montana

◯ = EASY　◯◯ = HARD　◯◯◯ = HARDER

BOLD AGGRESSOR
Yellow-headed Blackbird

Xanthocephalus xanthocephalus

Big, bright, and bossy, a **yellow-headed blackbird** male isn't about to share living quarters with another male of his own kind, let alone a red-winged blackbird. These blackbirds of the western states choose to nest on reeds in deeper waters, which better protects them from land predators.

The red-winged blackbirds would like these spots too, but tend to lose out to their tougher competitors. Fortunately, there's room for both species in the cattails—but not without a lot of singing, displaying, chasing, and fighting.

A yellow-headed blackbird perched on a cattail

A female yellow-headed blackbird feeding chicks

A male yellow-headed blackbird

Watch out!

A yellow-headed male will chase you away if you get too close to its basket-like nest, woven around reed stems. These daring birds have been known to strike hawks, crows, and even people.

MONTANA BIRD-FINDING TIPS

Montana	◯
Glacier	◯◯◯
Yellowstone	◯
Key features	Male—bright yellow head; female—muted yellow chest
Habitats	Marshes
Favorite foods	Seeds, insects
Seasons	Spring through summer in Montana; winter in the Southwest and Mexico

◯ = EASY   ◯◯ = HARD   ◯◯◯ = HARDER

SNEAKIEST INTRUDER
Red-winged Blackbird
Agelaius phoeniceus

"Konk-la-reeee!" A **red-winged blackbird** sings and flashes his scarlet shoulder badge to warn off a rival male. Meanwhile, another male sneaks into the cattails with his badge concealed, but is spotted and chased away. It's tough being king of a corner in the marsh. A top male may have 15 females nesting in his territory. Keeping trespassers out takes a lot of work!

Red-winged blackbird in flight

Flashing Badges
Red-winged blackbirds are easy to find perched on cattails in marshes across America. Their cheery *konk-la-ree* song is a welcome sign of spring. Take time to watch them closely. Are the males showing or hiding their badges? Covering a badge is a sly behavior—an intruding male is hoping to mate with a female that is in the top male's territory. The strategy works—sometimes half of the young in a dominant male's territory are not his own offspring.

Red-winged blackbird showing his badge

MONTANA BIRD-FINDING TIPS

Montana	○
Glacier	○
Yellowstone	○
Key features	Male—black with scarlet wing badge; female—brown striped, sparrowlike
Habitat	Cattail marshes
Favorite foods	Seeds, insects
Seasons	Year round in western part of the state; others winter south of Montana

○ = EASY   ○○ = HARD   ○○○ = HARDER

MOST ABSENT PARENT
Brown-headed Cowbird

Molothrus ater

A female **brown-headed cowbird** lays an egg in a warbler nest and flies off. The next day, she finds a lazuli bunting nest, pushes out the bunting egg, and replaces it with her own. Her goal? To trick other birds into raising cowbird chicks.

This works for cowbirds, but not for the warbler and bunting parents, who spend most of their time stuffing grasshoppers into a cowbird nestling twice the size of their own chicks. Sometimes, the only chick to survive is the cowbird.

Brown-headed cowbird

Brown-headed cowbirds on a bison

Buffalo Bird

Cowbirds evolved to follow bison, feeding on insects stirred up by the animals' hooves and laying eggs in other birds' nests so they could keep up with the wandering herds. Bison are now gone from most of the American plains, but cowbirds are more numerous than ever.

When American settlers cleared forests and brought in horses and cows to replace bison, the cowbirds moved into new places they had never lived before. They now invade the nests of more than 200 songbirds, including warblers, buntings, and vireos.

Free rides!

Yellow Warblers Fight Back

Yellow warblers evolved with cowbirds, so they recognize cowbird eggs. Too tiny to toss out a cowbird egg, the yellow warbler covers it by building a new nest on top of the old one. One female built a six-story nest before she was free of cowbird eggs!

MONTANA BIRD-FINDING TIPS

Montana	◯
Glacier	◯
Yellowstone	◯
Key features	Black body, glossy brown head, thick bill, dark eyes
Habitat	Grasslands, pastures, forest edges, suburbs
Favorite foods	Insects, grain
Seasons	Spring and summer in Montana; winter in the Southwest and Mexico
Viewing spot	Yellowstone National Park—near bison herds

◯ = EASY   ◯◯ = HARD   ◯◯◯ = HARDER

North American CHAMPION

LARGEST AND HEAVIEST NEST
Bald Eagle
Haliaeetus leucocephalus

Imagine a **bald eagle** nest that is 20 feet tall and a roomy 9½ feet across built high up in a tree. That was North America's largest bird nest, a two-story nest found in Florida in the 1940s. The heaviest bird nest record goes to a two-ton Ohio nest that fell down after eagles had nested there for 35 years.

Bald eagle

A nest might start off about five feet wide. The same eagle pair returns each year and adds more sticks. After they die, another pair takes over. The nest keeps growing over several generations until it becomes so heavy it breaks the supporting tree limb.

Room with a View

Bald eagles eat fish, so they choose nesting trees overlooking rivers or lakes. In Montana, they often select tall cottonwood trees with broken tops or strong forks to hold a stick platform. In the center of the stick pile is a cup-shaped, pizza-sized inner nest, lined with moss and feathers, where the chicks cuddle up.

National Symbol Success Story

Once endangered because of the insect pesticide DDT, bald eagle numbers are increasing and should continue rising if we keep our waters clean and we take care of eagle habitat. In the 1970s, Montana had only 12 nesting pairs. Today, there are more than 300 pairs.

Bald eagle nesting

MONTANA BIRD-FINDING TIPS

Montana	◯◯
Glacier	◯◯
Yellowstone	◯◯
Key features	Adult—white head and white tail feathers; Juvenile—mottled brown; will not have fully white head until five years old
Habitat	Forests along waterways
Favorite foods	Fish, ducks, dead animals
Seasons	Year round
Viewing spots	Glacier National Park's Lake McDonald and Saint Mary's Lake

◯ = EASY　◯◯ = HARD　◯◯◯ = HARDER

ROOKERY CHAMPION
Great Blue Heron

Ardea herodias

"…we found seven nests at the top of two tall pole-like cottonwoods, placed in the extremities of branches so thin that they would not bear the weight of even a small boy."

—Evelyn Cameron, Montana photographer, writing about herons on the Yellowstone River in 1906

Great blue heron feeding her chick

Birds of a feather nest together. At least this is true for **great blue herons,** which jam in one tall tree in a colony called a rookery. Rookeries range from a few nests to hundreds of nests. Herons often choose cottonwood trees on islands that offer protection from climbing predators like raccoons.

Rock-a-Bye Baby?

How can a thin branch hold a nest with two gawky heron chicks and their parents? Because herons are light, made up of mostly feathers and hollow bones. An adult is 4 feet tall but weighs just 5 pounds.

Great blue heron chicks

Babies on Board!

If you discover an active rookery, stay far away to avoid scaring a heron off its nest. The eggs or chicks may become food for bald eagles or ravens.

Rookery School

A young heron learns one of two fishing methods by copying adults:

- **Statue technique:** Stand still, neck at 45 degrees, wait until a fish swims by, and then stab it with a dagger-sharp bill.

- **Wade and stir technique:** Wade in water, force a fish from its hiding place, lunge, and snap.

Great blue heron rookery

Montana	○
Glacier	○ ○
Yellowstone	○ ○
Key features	Large, gray-blue body, long neck and legs; in flight folds its neck back on its shoulders
Habitat	Cottonwood and pine trees along streams, rivers, lakes, marshes
Favorite foods	Fish, frogs, gophers, mice, snakes, turtles
Seasons	Year round

○ = EASY   ○○ = HARD   ○○○ = HARDER

MUDDIEST NEST
Cliff Swallow

Petrochelidon pyrrhonota

The **cliff swallow** uses about 1,000 mouthfuls of mud to build its gourd-shaped nest that is attached to the side of a cliff or wall. The finished nest is snug and waterproof, has a handy entrance, and connects to its neighbor—a mud castle complex!

Building a mud nest is like laying bricks. First, the male attaches a shelf of mud balls to the wall. Then the male and female build up the sides and roof. To keep the nest from collapsing, they wait for each layer to dry before adding the next.

Cliff swallow chicks

Finishing Touches
Cliff swallow pairs finish their nests in about two weeks. Once the entry hole is complete, they line the inside with grasses and feathers—ready for the female to lay four to five creamy white eggs.

Swallow Mud Wallow
Cliff swallows flock to mud holes, darting down with their wings and tails held high to keep them out of the mud. They scoop up mud balls in their beaks and fly back to the colony, where nests can number in the thousands—especially in western states like Montana.

Are You My Mother?
At a cliff swallow colony in June, hungry chicks peer out of every hole, waiting for their parents to feed them. Adults can pick out their own chick's calls from the twittering. They can also recognize their chicks, because each bird has a different feather color and pattern.

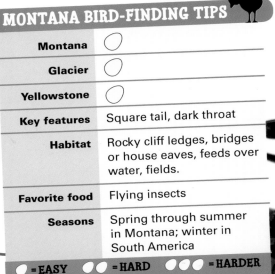
A colony of cliff swallows

Cliff swallows collecting mud

MONTANA BIRD-FINDING TIPS

Montana	◯
Glacier	◯
Yellowstone	◯
Key features	Square tail, dark throat
Habitat	Rocky cliff ledges, bridges or house eaves, feeds over water, fields.
Favorite food	Flying insects
Seasons	Spring through summer in Montana; winter in South America

◯ = EASY ◯◯ = HARD ◯◯◯ = HARDER

MESSIEST NEST
Black-billed Magpie

Pica hudsonia

If there were an award for the messiest nest, the **black-billed magpie** would win. A magpie nests looks like a big sloppy ball of sticks. Nevertheless, a magpie pair works hard on their masterpiece for more than six weeks, starting in early spring. The male selects and carries twigs to a sturdy fork in a tree and the female arranges them. Inside is a tidy cup nest lined with fur, hair, tiny roots, and grass that holds five to nine, one-inch speckled eggs.

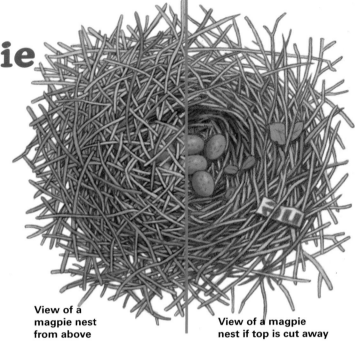

View of a magpie nest from above

View of a magpie nest if top is cut away

Nest-building Feat
How many flying trips does it take to build a magpie nest? One researcher counted a magpie pair that made 2,564 trips over 40 days. The finished nest can be as big as a doghouse (2 to 4 feet high).

Magpie Family Life
Magpies hang out in flocks and nest in colonies. Their noisy chatter and bold habits make them hard to miss. After the chicks leave their cozy nest (3 to 4 weeks after hatching), they follow their parents for a couple of months, learning to flip over objects to find food, scavenge meat scraps, and pick insects off the backs of grazing animals. The juveniles are easy to spot, because their tails are noticeably shorter than the adults.

Black-billed magpie

MONTANA BIRD-FINDING TIPS

Montana	◯
Glacier	◯
Yellowstone	◯
Key features	Black-and-white body, long tail, often flies in family groups
Habitat	Widespread in West, in towns, parks, and open country with scattered trees
Favorite foods	Insects, grain, small mammals, dead animals
Seasons	Year round

◯ =EASY ◯◯ =HARD ◯◯◯ =HARDER